STOP LIVING EXHAUSTED
& START LIVING **RESTORED**

Simplifying
Rest

A 28-day devotional
by Lisa Rowell

To Jesus who made it a point
to show us that naps
are perfectly okay for adults to take

And to Clay, Emmy, and Ellery
who remind me daily
of His abundant goodness

CONTENTS

WEEK 3: TRUST HIM   39

HOW TO START LIVING RESTED & RESTORED

Too many Christians are going through life on empty. We feel overwhelmed, overworked, and tired of being tired all of the time. This constant state of doing is undoing us. Maybe that's where you find yourself, too.

The Lord wants more for us—for YOU. In this 28-day devotional, my prayer is that you will begin to simplify and practice rest as part of your daily lifestyle by following His example of rest, looking to Him in every situation, trusting Him more, and choosing the rest He offers.

4 Simple Ways to Make the Most of These 4 Weeks
1. **Start small.** Each day is designed to take about 14 minutes. That's 1 percent of your day. Begin there.
2. **Rest on the seventh day.** On that day, put into practice resting in and with the Father with no agenda other than to be with Him. The seventh day includes a verse to help focus your thoughts.
3. **Pray.** Use the Simplifying Rest prayer on page 10 or follow the daily prayer prompts.
4. **Continue growing in your spiritual practice of rest.** Incorporate what you learn into your daily routines and rituals. See how God blesses your offering of time to lead you to grow closer to Him and to receive His restorative gift of rest.

The Lord's rest offers you reprieve from worry, stress, and striving. When you practice resting in Him, you can stop living exhausted and start living restored.

~Lisa

Simplifying Rest: THE PRAYER

Pray these words daily for the next 28 days and see where
He leads you. The Lord will meet you where you are. He
will slow you down and guide you to a place of rest.

Lord, I don't want to walk *ahead* of You.
I tend to veer off course and take unnecessary detours.
Please slow me down.

Lord, I don't want to walk *beside* You.
I fight to set the pace and move before You do.
Please slow me down.

Lord, I want to walk *behind* You.
I need to keep my eyes focused on You
and step where You lead.
Please slow me down.

Amen.

SIMPLIFYING REST

WEEK 1

FOLLOW HIS EXAMPLE

The Lord set rest apart from the beginning.
He made it sacred, holy. In His ministry on earth,
Jesus showed us how to both choose and practice rest
in the everyday. Walk in the footsteps of Jesus.
The Lord will lead you to a place of rest
and offer respite along the way.

DAY 1

GOD RESTED FIRST

In the beginning, God rested. The Creator of all things rested.

During those first seven days, God worked for six days and rested on the seventh day. On the first day, He created the heavens and earth, the waters and light. The second day saw the creation of the sky. On days three through six, the Lord filled the earth with the seas, dry ground, plants, animals, and people. Then, the Lord devoted an entire day to rest.

God worked and then He rested all day. He didn't work until lunch and then rest. He didn't wake up early to check on a few things before He took the day off. No. He took a full day of rest from His work. He blessed the day of rest and set it apart from the other days. The Lord gave us the perfect example of rest.

God designed us to follow suit but resting doesn't come easy when we live by the ways of the world. Our world defines us by our productivity and constantly tempts us to do more and work harder and longer. But, God invites us into the sacred space of resting with Him. He invites YOU. And, Friend, if the world didn't end when God rested, it certainly won't end if you take time to be still and rest.

"By the seventh day God had finished the work he had been doing; so on the seventh day he rested from all his work. And God blessed the seventh day and made it holy, because on it he rested from all the work of creating that he had done." (Genesis 2:2,3 NIV)

THINK ABOUT IT.

What are your thoughts about rest? When it comes to taking a full day of rest, in what ways do you buy into the world's idea of rest? Do you take a full day of rest consistently or do you work on your off days? What is your biggest hurdle to overcome in order to take a full day off each week?

RESPOND.

Thank God for the gift of rest and for showing you the need for rest from the beginning. Ask for His help in removing your biggest hurdle so you can follow His example of rest. Commit to Him (and yourself) to practice simplifying rest for the next 28 days.

PRAY.

Use the Simplifying Rest Prayer on page 10 or offer up your own words. Be intentional about using prayer as part of your restful practices over the next 28 days.

NOTES:

DAY 2

SLOW DOWN

During His ministry on earth, Jesus was known for a lot of things—being in a hurry wasn't one of them.

Jesus wasn't in a hurry to start His earthly ministry. He wasn't in a hurry to wake up from His nap even when His boat encountered a storm that scared the most experienced fishermen. He wasn't in a hurry to get to Lazarus even when his dear friend was dying. He wasn't in a hurry to keep walking to the next town even though people needed Him there.

Jesus slowed down to rest. He slowed down to spend time with His Father. He slowed down to invite His disciples to rest with Him. When Jesus felt tired, He slowed down to take a break.

Want to be more like Jesus? Slow down. Rest in the Lord. Trust His timing, His faithfulness, His goodness, and His plans for your life. Go at His pace, not your own.

"Slow down. Take a deep breath. What's the hurry? Why wear yourself out? Just what are you after anyway?" (Jeremiah 2:25 MSG)

Yes! Slow down. Take a deep breath and follow Jesus' example of rest.

THINK ABOUT IT.

What in your life feels so urgent that you believe you can't take the time to slow down and rest? How do you respond to people or situations when you are busy or rushing to the next place to be? What about those times when you make the decision to slow down?

RESPOND.

Ask the Lord to help you follow Jesus' example to slow down. Listen for any changes to your schedule or mindset that He might be asking you to make. Be obedient to what He reveals to you.

PRAY.

Use the Simplifying Rest Prayer on page 10 or offer up your own words. When you find yourself getting ahead of God, return to this prayer.

NOTES:

DAY 3

PERMISSION TO STOP

Jesus didn't die on the Cross for you to die to your work. Yes, God calls you to do His work, but that same God also invites you to rest from it. His purpose can be found in both.

Rest is one of God's gifts to you—resting in Him, in His creation, in His blessings, in His comfort. His gift of rest is not because of what you do. God freely offers you the gift of rest because you are His child. You are more than what you produce or whom you are raising or your billable hours or your grades. Your life was meant for something more than work.

The Lord knows your tendency to be *more* productive and instead of urging you to do it all, He calls you to take time to rest with Him. It's what Jesus did during His earthly ministry. He rested even though His schedule suggested that He keep pushing forward. Jesus' example gives you permission to stop.

The next time you feel overwhelmed with what needs to get done, create space to rest with Him. Instead of working overtime or late into the night, pause and follow Jesus' example of rest.

"Then, because so many people were coming and going that they did not even have a chance to eat, he said to them, 'Come with me by yourselves to a quiet place and get some rest.' " (Mark 6:31 NIV)

THINK ABOUT IT.
Do you rest well or do you barely rest? What does the Scripture from today reveal about Jesus' example of rest? How does His practice of rest differ from your own?

RESPOND.
Commit to following the example that Jesus gave us to stop and rest. Go to a quiet place and rest. Sit outside with the sun on your face or in your car with a worship song playing or wherever He leads you. Just go. Follow Him and His example.

PRAY.
Use the Simplifying Rest Prayer on page 10 or offer up your own words. Thank Him for showing you the importance of slowing down and stopping to rest.

NOTES:

DAY 4

THE RULES

When it comes to the concept of "rest," do you put rules around rest?

- I will rest after…
- Before I take a rest, I need to…
- I can't rest until I…
- I can only rest at the end of the day.
- I can only rest in the morning.
- I can only rest when the kids are sleeping.
- I will rest on vacation.
- I need to check my emails before I rest.
- _____.
- _____.

You aren't alone. Many Christians put all sorts of rules and regulations around rest that create barriers where the Lord created none.

Jesus didn't say, "Come to me after you clean the kitchen, respond to that text, answer those work emails, make the bed, decide what's for dinner, start a load of laundry, call that client, put the kids to bed, AND THEN I will give you rest."

Instead, Jesus simply said: " 'Come to me, all you who are weary and burdened, and I will give you rest.' " (Matthew 11:28 NIV)

The biblical example of rest that Jesus invites us to experience is simple. Tired? Rest. Overwhelmed? Rest. Go to Jesus and accept His invitation of rest. He puts no rules around rest for you to follow.

THINK ABOUT IT.

What rule or rules do you put around rest? Add them to the list on the previous page. Do those rules lead you to experience greater rest or do they add a hurdle to Jesus' invitation to rest?

RESPOND.

Ask God to help you break down the rules you've put in place for yourself about rest.

PRAY.

Use the Simplifying Rest Prayer on page 10 or offer up your own words. Thank Him for His open invitation to rest.

NOTES:

DAY 5

REST WHEN YOU'RE TIRED

Even Jesus felt tired at times. Scripture makes a point of telling us that He did.

If you've been a Christian for a bit, you might be familiar with the story of the Samaritan woman who met Jesus at a well in the middle of the day. She went at that time to avoid seeing her neighbors, who didn't approve of her lifestyle choices.

So why was Jesus there? Well, while on His way to another town, Jesus felt tired and He decided to take a break at the very place where the Samaritan woman went for water. Talk about simplifying rest! Jesus felt tired so He rested.

If Jesus hadn't taken the time to rest by the well, the Samaritan woman never would have met Him. If she never met Jesus, she never would have told her neighbors that the Messiah was at the well. And, if her neighbors never went to the well to see for themselves, they never would have experienced the Savior and believed, too.

It all started when Jesus recognized He felt tired and made the choice to rest in the middle of His workday. So, when you feel tired, rest. The Lord might be preparing you for something or someone. Rest can give you the breathing space to hear the quiet nudges of the Holy Spirit. If you don't take the time to rest, you might miss it in your busyness or exhaustion.

"Jesus, tired as he was from the journey, sat down by the well." (John 4:6b NIV)

THINK ABOUT IT.

Consider a time that you missed seeing an opportunity or how you could've helped someone because you felt tired. (You could have been tired emotionally, physically, spiritually, or mentally.) How do you think you would have approached the situation differently if you were rested instead?

RESPOND.

Thank God for using rest to prepare you. Ask for help in following Jesus' example to rest when you feel tired.

PRAY.

Use the Simplifying Rest Prayer on page 10 or offer up your own words. Learning to slow down and rest takes time. Extend the same grace to yourself that Jesus gave the Samaritan woman at the well.

NOTES:

DAY 6

WORK FROM A PLACE OF REST

When Jesus took time to rest, He still had work to do. People still needed Him. He still had places to be and still had miles to walk. Yet, Jesus made the choice to still Himself—to rest. He prayed. He went away by Himself. He napped. Yesterday, we looked at how He took a break in the middle of the day.

Taking a rest when you have work to do doesn't make you lazy. It makes you like Jesus. Think about this. What if His workload was precisely why He chose to rest? What if He took that nap or went away by Himself to pray so He could do the work? What if taking that rest allowed Him to continue the work from a place of rest and restoration rather than from a place of exhaustion?

What if you did the same? The quality of your own work and the way you treat your friends and family changes significantly when you are exhausted or burned out. It's not pretty or productive and it's definitely not life giving for anyone, including you.

But, when you take time to rest in Him and then turn towards your work and your relationships, you carry with you His restorative power. So, rest. If Jesus found time to rest, then you can, too. Choose to approach your work and your relationships from a place of restoration as if you are both serving and representing Him—because you are.

"Work willingly at whatever you do, as though you were working for the Lord rather than for people." (Colossians 3:23 NLT)

THINK ABOUT IT.

How have you used busyness or your workload or family responsibilities as an excuse for not fully resting? How do your conversations or your work go differently when you are well rested rather than exhausted? How do you treat yourself when you are overly tired?

RESPOND.

Commit to God (and yourself) to take time each day to rest so that you can approach your relationships and your work from a posture of restoration and rest not exhaustion.

PRAY.

Use the Simplifying Rest Prayer on page 10 or offer up your own words. Thank Jesus for His example of rest.

NOTES:

DAY 7

"My soul finds rest in God alone."

(Psalm 62:1a NIV)

It's the seventh day.

Follow His example and rest.

SIMPLIFYING REST

WEEK 2

LOOK TO HIM

This world provides daily reminders
of our brokenness. But, God is in the business
of restoration. Rest can be found when you keep
your eyes focused on Him and His daily reminders
of redemption, goodness, and love.

DAY 8

WHEN LIFE IS UNCERTAIN

We live in a time of more questions than answers, more fears and divisions than peace and unity. You don't need a list of all the ways this is true right now, but it's not new. We've been a mess since Chapter 3 of the story. That's when sin entered God's perfect creation.

Adam and Eve bit into the fruit in Genesis 3:6. While you know how the story ends, you are being called to live during this moment in history. But how do you find peace and rest when the brokenness of the world *feels* more personal to you at a given moment in time? How do you rest when uncertainty and divisions cause feelings of fear?

You can walk through the unknown by focusing on the known. You can look to God for His peace and rest. You can keep your eyes locked on Him and His promises. You can seek Him every day, every hour, and every second. He will always deliver you from your fears when you seek Him with your whole heart. And when you choose to seek Him, you are changed, even if your circumstances remain the same.

Psalm 34:4 NIV puts it this way: "I sought the LORD, and he answered me; he delivered me from all my fears."

When you look to God, He will deliver you, too. Turn your face away from fears and uncertainty and look instead at the Lord. Rest in His love for you. He will rescue you from your fears.

THINK ABOUT IT.

How does the brokenness of this world seem especially close to home for you right now? What fears do you struggle with during these uncertain times? How does this impact your ability to rest and be at peace?

RESPOND.

Thank God for His rescue plan in Jesus. Praise Him for His accessibility and the rest and peace that are found when you look to Him. Confess your fears to Him and ask for Him to deliver you from them.

PRAY.

Use the Simplifying Rest Prayer on page 10 or offer up your own words. His ways always lead you away from fears and towards rest and peace.

NOTES:

DAY 9

WHEN YOU ARE THE STORM

Jesus calmed the storm.

You might already know how the story goes. While Jesus rested after a long day of teaching, a furious storm raged around the boat carrying Him and His disciples. The waves broke over the boat threatening to sink it. In their fear, the professional fishermen Jesus recruited as His disciples ran to Him for help.

And Jesus calmed the storm. He said to the wind and waves: "Quiet! Be still!" (Mark 4:39 NIV) With those words, the storm stopped.

A common way to view this story is through the lens of trusting Jesus to see us through storms in our lives. And that's true, but can we be bravely honest with each other? Sometimes WE are that storm that surges. Sometimes we get caught up in our emotions. Sometimes we rage against battles that aren't ours to fight. Sometimes we find ourselves drowning in our own thoughts and actions and we lose sight of the One in control.

And you know what the Lord says to us—what the Lord says to YOU—in those moments? Essentially the same thing He said on the boat: "Be still, and know that I am God." (Psalm 46:10a NIV)

The Greek and Hebrew words used in those two passages are different but they carry similar meanings. *To cease. Calm down. Settle. Put a muzzle on it. Hold your peace.*

In Mark, the wind and the waves recognized the One who spoke and calmed down under His authority. When you, too, still yourself, recognize His greatness, and surrender yourself to His authority, you can rest knowing that He is in control.

So, be still. Take your eyes off the storm raging inside (or around) you and look to Him. Acknowledge His glory. Listen to His voice. Trust in Him. Hold on to Him. Rest in Him. Let Him do what only He can do. He will calm the storm, even if you are the storm that needs to settle down.

THINK ABOUT IT.
When in your life have you been the storm that rages in your thoughts, actions, or words? How have your thoughts, actions, or words threatened to wreck the rest and peace He offers? How do the storms you stir up impact your relationships?

RESPOND.
Confess the times you tend to be the storm. Ask for the Lord's help to remember to look to Him in those moments. Commit to practicing being still and looking to Him.

PRAY.
Use the Simplifying Rest Prayer on page 10 or offer up your own words as you intentionally make resting in Him a larger part of your life.

NOTES:

DAY 10

REMEMBER WHO HE IS

Not all rest comes from pouring into yourself with self-care. Rest also comes from looking to the Lord and pouring out praises to Him.

Think about the overwhelming peace and joy you experience after a powerful worship service or when you hear a worship song that seems written especially for you. Yes! Worship can leave you rested and joyful, seen and hopeful.

Lasting rest can be found when you daily—and consistently—look to the Lord and pour out praise offerings to Him. Not because of what He can do for you but because of Who He is.

- He is good.
- He is in control.
- He is merciful.
- He is compassionate.
- He is just.
- He is kind.
- He is LOVE.
- He is Savior!

"Through Jesus, therefore, let us continually offer to God a sacrifice of praise—the fruit of lips that openly profess his name." (Hebrews 13:15 NIV)

THINK ABOUT IT.

How has worshipping the Lord given you a sense of rest and peace? Consider a church service or other sacred experience that left you feeling full of the Holy Spirit. How did that impact the rest of that day or night?

RESPOND.

Worship Him right now. Profess to Him who He is in your life. If you aren't sure where to start, pick one worship song and listen to it. Sing! Or proclaim out loud the bullet points on the previous page.

PRAY.

Use the Simplifying Rest Prayer on page 10 or offer up your own words. Look to Him to lead you to a place of rest.

NOTES:

DAY 11

BE GROUNDED IN WHAT GOD IS DOING

Being a Christian doesn't exclude you from falling prey to the *What If* game. Sometimes it might seem like just as you sit down for a break or get in bed for the night, your mind wanders into a screening of the latest *What If* blockbuster movie starring You. And, Friend, I bet you could be nominated for Best Screenplay based on the scenarios you devise.

So, how do you stop looking for the What Ifs that stir up anxiety and unrest in your mind and instead start looking to God and His rest? Here's one way. Ground yourself in what God is doing in the moment.

Matthew 6:34 from *The Message* puts it this way: "Give your entire attention to what God is doing right now, and don't get worked up about what may or may not happen tomorrow. God will help you deal with whatever hard things come up when the time comes."

Let's get super practical right now. When you get caught up in the What Ifs, try this grounding technique, sometimes called the 5-4-3-2-1 technique. Take a deep breath and hold it for 5 seconds. Breathe out for 5 seconds and then repeat while also naming the following:

- Name 5 things you can see around you.
- Name 4 things you can touch around you.
- Name 3 things you can hear around you.
- Name 2 things you can smell around you.
- Name 1 thing you can taste.

Use this grounding technique to help you look to God and focus on what He is doing right now rather than your anxious What If thoughts. All of the What Ifs keep you distracted from how God and His rest are available to you at any time. By intentionally shifting your attention to His presence in your life all around you in the moment, His rest and peace can be more easily experienced.

THINK ABOUT IT.
What are your most frequent What If thoughts about? How do those thoughts get in the way of experiencing His rest?

RESPOND.
Ask for God's help to keep your attention on what He is doing in your life today. Practice the 5-4-3-2-1 technique several times this week.

PRAY.
Use the Simplifying Rest Prayer on page 10 or offer up your own words. Slowing down to follow Him keeps your focus on Him rather than your What If thoughts.

NOTES:

DAY 12

WHEN STRESS & WORRY KEEP YOU UP AT NIGHT

Stress and worry feed us lies about the limits of what the Lord can do and keep us distracted from His goodness, His faithfulness, His love for us, and His gift of rest.

God knows that worried thoughts are a common war tactic of Satan. Maybe that's why He tells us over and over again not to be worried or anxious about anything. We need those reminders, too, because we are a pretty forgetful lot.

So, here's another reminder: The Lord will not abandon you to your worried thoughts. He won't leave you alone with your stress. He offers you rest from them—even at 3am. When your anxious or stressful thoughts fight against sleep, the Lord invites you to rest in the shadow of His wings and remember Who He is and who you are in Him.

The next time stress and worry shake you awake think of Him. Praise Him. Breathe in and exhale out slowly while telling Him: I remember You. (Or: HELP ME remember You.) And repeat. The Lord will meet you in that moment and give you rest.

"On my bed I remember you;
I think of you through the watches of the night.
Because you are my help,
I sing in the shadow of your wings.
I cling to you;
your right hand upholds me." (Psalm 63:6–8 NIV)

THINK ABOUT IT.

What are three things you know to be true about God? (Need help? Look at the list on Day 10.) How have you personally experienced those three characteristics of God?

RESPOND.

Look to Him and breathe in and exhale out while saying: I remember You. Or try saying what you know to be true about Him, such as: You are good. You are kind. You are trustworthy. You are loving. You watch over me and work things out for good.

Write a reminder to yourself and leave it next to your bed for the nights you need help looking to Him.

PRAY.

Use the Simplifying Rest Prayer on page 10 or offer up your own words. Keep practicing slowing down and focusing on what you know to be true about God.

NOTES:

DAY 13

WHEN YOU ARE LOST

It doesn't matter which app you use—Google Maps, Waze, Apple Maps...or even a map stuffed in your glove compartment—it's still easy to get lost, to miss the turn, to get distracted by roadside attractions, or to give in to the monotony of the interstate.

It's easy to get lost in life, too.

Work, school, and your relationships can distract you. You might find yourself caught up in what others think about you, what people post on social media or binge watching the latest, greatest thing. Maybe you give in to the monotony of weekly routines. Then one day you look up and realize that you've lost sight of God and His purpose and path for your life.

It's okay. Being lost isn't a permanent situation. If you find yourself lost, God makes it simple to find the way. Look to Him and ask for directions. Rest with Him a while and allow Him to recalculate your direction.

Jeremiah 6:16 NIV puts it this way: "Stand at the crossroads and look; ask for the ancient paths, ask where the good way is, and walk in it, and you will find rest for your souls."

When you take a rest with Him, He directs your steps back towards walking in His purpose for your life. You may feel lost but you can trust that the Lord always knows exactly where you are.

THINK ABOUT IT.

In what area of your life do you feel like you've lost your way? How does this impact your ability to fully experience His rest?

RESPOND.

Confess to God where you feel lost. Ask Him to point out the next step for you to take towards Him and His rest. Then take it.

PRAY.

Use the Simplifying Rest Prayer on page 10 or offer up your own words. If you find yourself ahead of God or lost, stop and turn towards Him. He is always near.

NOTES:

DAY 14

"You will seek me and find me when you seek me with all your heart."

(Jeremiah 29:13 NIV)

It's the seventh day.

Look to Him and rest.

SIMPLIFYING REST

WEEK 3

TRUST HIM

The Lord never changes. Though the world may waver
and your circumstances fluctuate, you can rest
with confidence knowing that the same God
who chose Mary, led Moses, rescued Rahab,
and redeemed Paul invites you to rest in and with Him.
Trust that He chooses you, leads you, rescues you,
and redeems you, too.

DAY 15

HE REIGNS

Forget about who wears the pants in your family. Instead ask yourself: *Who wears the crown?*

It's easy enough to read in Scripture or sing out during a worship song "He reigns." However, it's another thing entirely to choose to take the ill-fitting crown off your own head, kneel down, and submit to His authority on a daily basis in all areas of your life.

But, you know what happens when you participate in a daily spiritual coronation of the King? You can rest. When you look to Him and trust that He sits on the throne over all creation, over all situations, over everything in your life and in the world, you can rest secure. You can stop fighting to be in control of the things and situations out of your control and trust His authority.

You can trust Him to never abdicate His throne, to never abandon you, to never stop fighting for you—even in those moments when *you* fight against Him and His authority.

The Lord doesn't need a daily reminder of Who He is, but this practice sure helps you to keep your life and purpose and the cycles of worldly conflict and suffering in perspective. You can rest assured when you trust His sovereignty daily.

"I keep my eyes always on the LORD.
With him at my right hand, I will not be shaken.
Therefore my heart is glad and my tongue rejoices;
my body also will rest secure." (Psalm 16:8,9 NIV)

THINK ABOUT IT.

In which areas of your life do you most resist giving God control? Your finances? Your career? Parenting? Your marriage? Your dreams? What step can you take today to trust Him in that area?

RESPOND.

Repeat the Scripture from today out loud. Commit to the words you are saying. Write them down and repeat them every morning this week. Ask Him to help you let go of the crown and trust His sovereignty.

PRAY.

Use the Simplifying Rest Prayer on page 10 or offer up your own words. Trust that the King is leading you.

NOTES:

DAY 16

HE KNOWS BEST

You can't make me do anything!

On the day my then four-year-old shouted those words to me, I knew that the gig was up. She was right and I told her so. I couldn't *make* her do anything, but it was rest time and she could choose to trust that I knew what was best for her or she could choose not to rest and deal with the consequences of her actions.

What do you think she picked? Or better yet: what do YOU choose when your Father tells you it's rest time? Do you argue? Ignore Him? Keep doing what you're doing? Put resting off for when you *feel* like it? Or do you trust that He knows what is best for you? Do you trust that He sees your need for rest even when you don't (or won't)?

Put fresh eyes on this famous passage: "The LORD is my Shepherd, I lack nothing. He makes me lie down in green pastures." (Psalm 23:1,2 NIV)

The Shepherd *makes* the sheep lie down. Sheep are defenseless animals and they need to feel at peace and completely safe from predators before they can even think about resting in an open field. They need to know that they can trust their shepherd.

That's exactly what the Prince of Peace—Your Good Shepherd—offers you when you look to Him and trust Him. You can trust that He will watch over you. You can trust that He will protect you. You can trust that He knows when you need rest and will lead you to a safe place right next to Him.

THINK ABOUT IT.

How do you fight against rest? What consequences do you suffer when you choose not to rest? How does your lack of rest impact your relationships? Your work or school? The way you handle your emotions or the emotions of others?

RESPOND.

Ask God to help you stop fighting against His rest and trust that He knows best.

PRAY.

Use the Simplifying Rest Prayer on page 10 or offer up your own words. Trust that His pace and path is best and will lead to rest.

NOTES:

DAY 17

HE IS IN CONTROL

How do you amplify rest in your life while living in a culture transfixed with amplifying unrest? How do you turn off anxious thoughts and fears when dealing with health issues, financial difficulties, hurting relationships, racism, or other daily reminders of the world's brokenness and your own inability to make everything okay all of the time?

It's simple but not easy. Look to God and trust that He is in control. He will lead you through this and offer you rest and peace when you follow His example, look to Him, and trust Him in every situation.

When you free yourself from straining to be in control, you can stop holding your breath in anticipation of what might happen next. You can exhale and rest in the truth that He is in control so you can stop trying to be. Let me say that a different way: **HE'S GOT THIS** (whatever THIS is for you right now). You can trust Him.

"If God hadn't been there for me,
   I never would have made it.
The minute I said, 'I'm slipping, I'm falling,'
   your love, GOD, took hold and held me fast.
When I was upset and beside myself,
   you calmed me down and cheered me up."
(Psalm 94:17–19 MSG)

THINK ABOUT IT:
At what time or in which situations have you found yourself struggling to fully trust that God is in control? What about a time or situation when you fully trusted that God was in control? What helped you to fully trust Him?

RESPOND:
Confess your fears and anxieties to God. Go ahead. You can trust Him. Ask Him to help you develop a deeper trust. When you start to slip into your fears or anxieties, practice this breathing technique. Take deep breaths in and exhale slowly. Say the following either out loud or silently:

Breathe in: I trust You.
Breathe out: You are in control.

PRAY.
Use the Simplifying Rest Prayer on page 10 or offer up your own words. Trust that God is always in control and He will not be surprised by what you encounter today or tomorrow.

NOTES:

DAY 18

HE LISTENS & TENDS TO YOU

Do you ever argue with God over what He is leading you to do? Maybe you aren't always obedient right away. You ask questions. You hear His response and ask more questions (or pretend you didn't hear His answer). You push back. Try to negotiate better terms that seem more agreeable. You cry out in frustration when He doesn't seem to understand just how exhausted you are from doing what He asks you to do. You just want to give up.

You aren't alone. Consider the story of Elijah. At the height of his ministry, Elijah wanted to call it quits. He was done, exhausted, emotionally defeated, lonely, and discouraged in his work. And He ran—not from God—but to God to quit. What did the Lord do? He listened. He touched him. He fed him and He offered Elijah rest.

" 'I have had enough, LORD,' he said. 'Take my life; I am no better than my ancestors.' Then he lay down under the bush and fell asleep. All at once an angel touched him and said, 'Get up and eat.' He looked around, and there by his head was some bread baked over hot coals, and a jar of water. He ate and drank and then lay down again." (1 Kings 19:4b-6 NIV)

The offer of rest isn't just an Old Testament offer. The Lord offers you rest, too. When you are done, exhausted, emotionally defeated, lonely, and discouraged in the work the Lord calls you to do, run to Him—not from Him. Trust Him with your struggles. Trust that He will listen and tenderly care for you—and give you rest.

THINK ABOUT IT.

What area of your life is draining you? Parenting? Your job? Caring for an aging parent? Your marriage? Your health? Your bills? How might retreating and resting in the Lord help give you strength?

RESPOND.

Talk with the Lord honestly about the areas of your life that drain you. Write those areas down and then tape them to your bathroom mirror. Keep the conversation going with the Lord. Trust that He will listen and tend to your needs. Open your eyes and ears for the Lord's response of help and rest.

PRAY.

Use the Simplifying Rest Prayer on page 10 or offer up your own words. Trust that He will care for you just like He did Elijah.

NOTES:

DAY 19

HE CREATED YOU WITH A PURPOSE

The Lord created you with intention—*with* purpose and *for* a purpose. Be still with that for a moment. Accept the truth of those words. He could have created anyone and He chose to create you.

So, be gentle with yourself and the person the Lord created you to be. Nurture and water your dreams, your giftings, those hopes buried in your heart that you keep hidden with the busyness of life.

Give yourself space and permission to rest in Him and His purpose for you. Allow the spiritual gifts He gave you to be active in the everyday moments of living. He will present you with ways to use those gifts for His purposes. Trust Him.

Listen for Him in those silent spaces where your prayers pause in mid-sentence or when your day and mind quiet. The Lord whispers to you there His words of resurrection and rest.

When you hear from the Lord, trust His purpose for your life. Let Him reveal to you more of what that looks like in your everyday moments and relationships. Be the person the Lord created you to be. Walk with Him in confidence, knowing that in Him, your purpose will be fulfilled.

"I cry out to God Most High, to God who will fulfill his purpose for me." (Psalm 57:2 NLT)

THINK ABOUT IT.

How does striving to be someone you are not impact your rest? How does busyness and saying YES to every opportunity distract you from fully using your spiritual gifts or talents?

RESPOND.

Say these statements aloud, write them down, or take a photo and make it your lock screen.

- Lord, You created me with intention. I trust you.
- Lord, You created me *with* a purpose and *for* a purpose. I trust you.
- Lord, I find Your rest when I trust both Your purpose for my life and Your timing.

PRAY.

Use the Simplifying Rest Prayer on page 10 or offer up your own words. Trust His direction and pace for your life.

NOTES:

DAY 20

HE IS ALWAYS AT WORK

Winter shows us that even nature needs time to rest and retreat to its roots. While we can't see what God is doing to the trees, we trust that spring will come. We don't need to see Him working beneath the surface to know that He will bring the ground to flower in the spring. Instead, we remember from experience how winter makes way for spring.

"See! The winter is past; the rains are over and gone. Flowers appear on the earth; the season of singing has come…" (Song of Songs 2:11,12 NIV)

So, then why do we feel anxious or abandoned when we can't see what He is doing beneath the surface and out of sight during our own winter seasons? Why do we accept the cycles of retreating and resting and blooming and growing only in the Lord's creation of nature and fail to see the application in His creation of us?

To put it simply: We forget.

Our minds become dull to the memories of His deliverance in the past. We forget how He drew us close to His side when we struggled as a way to prepare our hearts and minds for a new direction or an answered prayer. We lose track of the times when we became rooted both in His Word and in prayer waiting with expectant hope for deliverance, for a fruitful season.

However, Friend, living from a place of rest means looking backward and remembering all that God has done for you in the past and trusting Him with your future. It means resting in confidence that He is always at work in your life, even if you can't see how He is preparing a way. Look at the trees and imagine how much more glorious His plans are for you! You, too, can abide in His truth that the season of singing will come.

THINK ABOUT IT.
How do you know that winter won't last forever? How do you feel when you see the first signs of spring? What lessons did the Lord teach you during a more recent winter season in your own life?

RESPOND.
Write down the lessons the Lord taught you from above or create a short video to your future self so you won't forget. Thank the Lord for always being at work, even when you can't see it. Admit that the next time you go through a winter season you might forget that He is still working things out for good. Ask for His help to remember so that your trust in Him can strengthen and you can rest.

PRAY.
Use the Simplifying Rest Prayer on page 10 or offer up your own words. Trust Him to lead you to a place of rest, even during a winter season.

NOTES:

DAY 21

**"He is my refuge and my fortress,
my God, in whom I trust."**

(Psalm 91:2 NIV)

It's the seventh day.

Trust Him and rest.

SIMPLIFYING REST

WEEK 4

CHOOSE HIS REST

The Lord offers you rest. However, He doesn't force you to accept it. You must make the choice for yourself, every day. When you accept His invitation to step under His wing, His rest and peace cover you.

DAY 22

A DAY OF REST

Sunday—we get one each week all year, every year. The Sabbath is a whole day of rest created by God and set aside and made holy by Him. Although the Lord, Himself, rested on the seventh day, He created this day for us.

So, choose to take the day. Maybe it's not a Sunday for you. Maybe it doesn't look like a day off from work for you. But take the day…or take the hour each week. Take the rest He created for you.

- Take it to follow His example of rest.
- Take it to rest, worship, and re-center your focus on Him.
- Take it to trust Him with your fears, anxieties, and grief.
- Take it to praise Him for His goodness and faithfulness.
- Take it to proclaim Him the Lord of your life.
- Take it to remind yourself He is in control.
- Take it to thank Him for making REST part of how He loves you.

"Then he said to them, 'The Sabbath was made for man, not man for the Sabbath.' " (Mark 2:27 NIV)

THINK ABOUT IT.

What gets in the way of you choosing to take a Sabbath each week? How is your week different when you do take a day of rest?

RESPOND.

Commit to taking a Sabbath each week for the next four weeks. However you chose to rest, add it to your calendar. Tell someone else about your commitment to choose rest.

PRAY.

Use the Simplifying Rest Prayer on page 10 or offer up your own words. Thank Him for making rest part of how He loves and leads you.

NOTES:

DAY 23

MAKE REST A PRIORITY

The world holds a narrow view of rest that focuses on self-care rituals and vacations. This perspective puts rest in the luxury item column and implies that rest needs ideal circumstances to occur.

But how do you rest during those imperfect moments? What about rest when your world breaks? When someone you love dies? When a relationship ends? When a diagnosis arrives? When natural disasters and destruction strike? When violence, injustice, and suffering escalate in the world, in your community, or in your own home?

How do you rest then? Why even make it a priority when it feels like a luxury to pause in the middle of the pain to rest?

In the moments when your world breaks (or the world breaks you), that's when you need rest the most. And not the kind of rest found in a hammock on a tropical island, but the rest found in the Lord. The rest found in Him is a necessity not a luxury.

When you choose to rest in Him and His promises for a future beyond your current sufferings, He will hold you steady. When life threatens to shake you to your core, the Lord will put your feet on solid ground when you choose to rest in Him.

You can choose to see rest as the world does—as a luxury item to indulge in under the perfect circumstances. Or you can choose to see rest as the Lord does—a time to trust in Him and be strengthened by Him.

"I might rest in the day of trouble...
Though the fig tree may not blossom,
Nor fruit be on the vines;
Though the labor of the olive may fail,
And the fields yield no food;
Though the flock may be cut off from the fold,
And there be no herd in the stalls—
Yet I will rejoice in the LORD,
I will joy in the God of my salvation.
The LORD God is my strength."
(Habakkuk 3:16b–19a NKJV)

THINK ABOUT IT.

On a scale from 1 to 10, how would you rate the way you view (and practice) rest? 1 is you view rest as a luxury item that needs the perfect circumstances. 10 is you rest fully in the Lord all of the time, regardless of your present circumstances.

RESPOND.

Ask the Lord to continue to strengthen your understanding of the kind of rest He offers and to help you choose His rest in the everyday moments.

PRAY.

Use the Simplifying Rest Prayer on page 10 or offer up your own words. Choose to let Him lead you to experience the fullness of His rest.

NOTES:

DAY 24

TO DO OR TO BE

Let me get right to the point. Your To Be list matters more than your To Do list.

- Be with Him.
- Be forgiving.
- Be kind.
- Be loving.
- Be patient.
- Be courageous.
- Be identified as His follower.
- Be at rest under His wings.
- Be _____.
- Be _____.

While the world tells you to work longer and harder, He invites you to be at rest with Him. One way will break you until you have nothing left to give. One way will restore you so you can finish the work. You can choose to prioritize DOING or you can choose to prioritize BEING.

When you keep your focus on the person He calls you To Be, you can approach what He calls you To Do from a place of joyful rest and restoration.

"Because you are my help, I sing in the shadow of your wings." (Psalm 63:7 NIV)

THINK ABOUT IT.

Do you choose to focus more attention on your To Do list or your To Be list? Which list is easier for you? Which list helps you grow to be more like Jesus? Which list brings you more rest?

RESPOND.

Write down a To Be list for yourself. Give yourself a daily reminder that the Lord cares about the person you are becoming while the world focuses on what you are doing. Make the daily choice to focus on *becoming* rather than on *doing*.

PRAY.

Use the Simplifying Rest Prayer on page 10 or offer up your own words. Choose to be at rest under the Lord's wings and ask Him to help you become more like Jesus.

NOTES:

DAY 25

TO REST IN THE SHADOW

Shadows usually imply lurking peril. Danger and destruction seem to wait on the fringes of the light. But Psalm 91:1 NIV offers a different take. The Scripture declares: "Whoever dwells in the shelter of the Most High will rest in the shadow of the Almighty."

The Lord's shadow offers rest from danger. The only way to be in the shadow of the Lord is to choose to be close to Him—close enough where He casts a shadow over you. It's not a place to visit occasionally on a Sunday morning either. He wants you to plant roots and settle down there.

When you choose to live in His shadow, you can lean on Him while you release your burdens, your struggles, your fears, your failures, and your sins. You can ask for and receive His forgiveness. You can recover your strength because He is the very source of it.

Choosing to rest in His shadow isn't a passive experience. It is one of movement. The Lord is always leading you to take a step in faith. When He moves, so does His shadow. When you choose to follow Him closely each day, you can rest in Him and move wherever He leads.

Resting in His shadow is a daily choice.

THINK ABOUT IT.

When do you or when did you feel closest to God? How does your closeness to God (or lack of closeness) change the way you approach your day and experience rest?

RESPOND.

Ask for His help to stay close. Seek His guidance in keeping your eyes and heart open for when He moves so you can choose to stay close enough to rest in His shadow.

PRAY.

Use the Simplifying Rest Prayer on page 10 or offer up your own words. Choose to slow down and stay under the protection of the Almighty's shadow.

NOTES:

DAY 26

EXPERIENCE THE HOLINESS OF REST

From the beginning, rest was holy. From the beginning, rest was set apart. From the beginning, rest was blessed.

God rested first. Then later His Son gave us a real-world example of how to manage a busy work schedule and rest. Our work and our rest both matter to God, but He made only one holy.

Yes. The Lord commands us to keep the Sabbath, but He doesn't force us to experience the holiness of rest. We—you—must choose for yourself to experience it, to enter into it. You can elect to go through the outward motions of rest without choosing to seek the inward shelter of His embrace for rest. Or you can decide to humble yourself, cultivate a quiet heart, and seek the holy ground found when you approach Him and accept His gift of rest.

David put it this way in Psalm 131:2,3 NLT: "I have calmed and quieted myself, like a weaned child who no longer cries for its mother's milk. Yes, like a weaned child is my soul within me. O Israel, put your hope in the Lord—now and always."

Notice that David wrote, "I have calmed and quieted myself," not "The Lord calmed and quieted me." David made the choice to still himself and to trust the Lord. A weaned child is content to seek her mother's arms simply to be held, to feel safe, and to rest. You can experience the holiness of His rest, too, when you choose to seek the same with your Father.

THINK ABOUT IT.

What gets in your way of experiencing the holiness of rest?
How does your outlook shift when you fully give in to and
accept God's gift of rest?

RESPOND.

Choose to calm yourself throughout the day and accept His
rest. Practice right now. Proclaim out loud: I put my hope
in you, Lord.

PRAY.

Use the Simplifying Rest Prayer on page 10 or offer up your
own words. Choose to follow His lead and recognize that
you walk on holy ground behind Him.

NOTES:

DAY 27

REMEMBER WHAT GOD DID

Rest can be found when you remember God's big picture of rescue and redemption and rest. It's been His plan for His children all along. The Bible includes example after example. But, you must make the choice to remember. The world would have you forget. Your flesh tries to keep your focus on your present circumstances and not on God's view of eternity.

- When you remember how He rescued you in the past, you can rest with assurance that He will make a way again.
- When you remember how He provided for you in the past, you can rest with confidence that He will continue to take care of your needs.
- When you remember how He carried you through grief and suffering, you can rest in peace knowing that His arms are always open for you.
- When you remember that He created the flowers to follow the winter, you can rest with expectant hope that He has not abandoned you to your current season (no matter how stark and barren).
- When you remember how He sacrificed His Son, you can rest with conviction that Jesus' death offers eternal atonement for your sins.
- When you remember His Resurrection, you can rest with joy knowing that in the end LIFE and LIGHT and LOVE cannot be defeated.

"I will remember the deeds of the LORD; yes, I will remember your miracles of long ago." (Psalm 77:11 NIV)

THINK ABOUT IT.
How has the Lord rescued you in the past? Answered a prayer? Brought you comfort? Provided for your needs? Mended a relationship? Look back at Day 20 and read what you wrote or watch your video.

RESPOND.
Thank Him for all of the ways He cared for you in the past. Ask for His help to never forget, especially in those times when you feel overwhelmed or stressed about your current situation or circumstances. Choose to accept the gift of rest He offers you.

PRAY.
Use the Simplifying Rest Prayer on page 10 or offer up your own words. Choose to remember that following His example, looking to Him, and trusting Him will always lead to rest.

NOTES:

DAY 28

"The Lord reigns."

(Psalm 93:1 NIV)

It's the seventh day.

Choose to rest in and with the King.

NOW WHAT?

Rest is a spiritual practice. The more you choose to spend time resting in and with Him, the better you can become at living your life from a place of rest and restoration. The Lord invites you to rest with Him throughout your day. How do you do that? Keep practicing!

- Practice following His example.
- Practice looking to Him in every situation.
- Practice putting your trust in Him.
- Practice choosing the rest He offers.

And, Friend, extend grace to yourself. Practice doesn't mean perfection. It just means you commit to the process of learning to be more like Jesus every single day. So, keep practicing ways to simplify rest in your life. Start right now.

**Look up. Breathe deeply and simply say:
Thank You.**

ABOUT THE AUTHOR

As a writer and speaker, Lisa Rowell uses
her words to make our world a more peaceful place.
Her heart beats for early childhood education, encouraging
women, and pointing people to Jesus. Through the years,
her work has been included in *Parenting, BabyTalk*, and
Southern Living magazines, in numerous Bible study and
devotional collaborations and as a ghostwriter
for popular consumer brands.

She currently lives in the Atlanta area
with her husband, Clay, and their two daughters.

Website: lisarowell.com
Instagram: @lisarowellwrites